Brighter Baking
with
m&m's ®
BRAND
Chocolate Mini Baking Bits

helpful hints for successful baking

Use butter or margarine or solid vegetable shortening as directed. The recipes developed by the M&M/MARS Kitchens suggest the use of butter, margarine and/or shortening in varying amounts and combinations. For the best flavor and texture, use the types suggested in each recipe. Substituting one type for another can produce undesirable baked goods. Do not use vegetable oil spreads, diet, lite, soft, whipped or liquid versions of butter or margarine. These products perform differently in baking and may cause unsatisfactory results.

Measure ingredients carefully. Metal or plastic cups are intended for dry ingredients like flour and sugar; graduated glass or plastic cups with spouts should be used for liquids. If you use a liquid measuring cup for flour, you may get an extra tablespoon or more per cup. This could make cookies hard and dry. To measure flour, lightly spoon it from the canister into the measuring cup and level it with the straight edge of a spatula or knife. Do not tap or shake the cup to level it. When measuring brown sugar, pack it firmly into the dry measuring cup so that it holds its shape when removed from the cup.

Preheat your oven for at least 10 to 15 minutes before starting to bake. Oven temperatures can vary as much as 50 degrees. Check the oven temperature with an oven thermometer to assure the dial setting is accurate. If no oven thermometer is available, try a test cookie; if it spreads too much, the temperature may be too high.

Bake one sheet of cookies at a time. Place the rack in the center of the oven. If you put two baking sheets in the oven at one time, it is best to switch their positions halfway through the baking time.

Make cookies that are in the same batch the same size and shape. Arrange cookie dough in even rows on the cookie sheets so cookies bake evenly. Do not leave large empty spaces as cookies will tend to burn.

Allow cookie sheets to cool thoroughly between batches. Putting dough onto hot cookie sheets may cause the cookies to spread and brown too much around the edges.

Use flat cookie sheets or those with very low edges. Shiny, heavy gauge aluminum cookie sheets are best; dark cookie sheets may cause overbrowning. For best results, the cookie sheets should be 1 to 2 inches smaller on all sides than the oven rack to allow proper air circulation.

Prepare cookie sheets and baking pans as directed before you begin to mix the recipe. If light greasing is suggested, use vegetable oil spray or a small amount of solid vegetable shortening. Do not use butter or margarine as it may burn on cookie sheets. Using parchment paper (available in many supermarkets and specialty stores) instead of greasing cookie sheets will help reduce clean-up.

Allow cookies to cool slightly before removing them from the pan. As soon as cookies are rigid enough to move without breaking, transfer them to a wire cooling rack to cool completely. Do not leave cookies on the cookie sheet; they continue to bake before they begin to cool.

Store cookies in tightly covered containers. Be sure cookies are completely cooled before storing. Do not store crisp and soft cookies together—the crisp ones will soften. To preserve each cookie's unique flavor, it is best to store each variety of cookies in its own container.

Freeze baked cookies for always-ready snacks. Double wrap cooled cookies in plastic wrap or plastic storage bags and store in freezer for up to 3 months. To thaw, remove cookies from freezer, unwrap and place cookies in single layer on wire racks for 15 to 30 minutes. Store unused cookies in tightly covered container.

3

fun facts about

m&m's®
BRAND

- "M&M's"® Chocolate Mini Baking Bits were first introduced in 1992. One-third the size of "M&M's,"® these candies are a colorful alternative to baking morsels.

- Well over 300 million "M&M's"® Chocolate Candies are consumed every day in the United States!

- From 1940 to 1950 there were violet "M&M's"® Plain Chocolate Candies! (Violet was then replaced by tan.)

- "M&M's"® Chocolate Candies rocketed into space with our first space shuttle astronauts! "M&M's"® are now on permanent display as part of the space food exhibit at the National Air & Space Museum of the Smithsonian Institute in Washington, D.C.

- When "M&M's"® Peanut Chocolate Candies were introduced in 1954, they only came in brown! Red, yellow, orange and green "M&M's"® were introduced in 1960.

- The "M&M's"® Chocolate Candies slogan, "The milk chocolate melts in your mouth...not in your hand"® was introduced in 1954!

- The M's were not printed on "M&M's"® until 1950! The M's were originally printed in black and were changed in 1954 to the white M's you see today.

- "M&M's"® were originally sold in a paper tube for five cents!

- "M&M's"® Chocolate Candies were part of the soldiers' "C" rations in World War II. They are also a part of today's MRE's (Meals Ready to Eat) and were enjoyed by the men and women who served our country in Desert Storm/Desert Shield and the Bosnian Peacekeeping Mission.

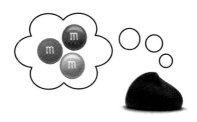

Did you know chocolate chips dream in color?

M&M's"® Mini Baking Bits are just like chocolate chips—they're small, available in semi-sweet or milk chocolate and they're just right for baking. Only difference is, they're a lot more colorful. So from now on, use them in any recipe that calls for chocolate chips. Cause it's bad enough you have to dream in black and white, let alone bake in it.

Contact us on the Internet http://www.m-ms.com
© Mars, Incorporated 1996

cookie jar favorites

colorific chocolate chip cookies

Everybody's favorite is made more fun with the addition of "M&M's"® Semi-Sweet Chocolate Mini Baking Bits!

1 cup (2 sticks) butter or margarine, softened
⅔ cup granulated sugar
½ cup firmly packed light brown sugar
1 large egg
1 teaspoon vanilla extract
2 cups all-purpose flour
¾ teaspoon baking soda
¾ teaspoon salt
1¾ cups "M&M's"® Semi-Sweet Chocolate Mini Baking Bits
¾ cup chopped nuts, optional

Preheat oven to 375°F. In large bowl cream butter and sugars until light and fluffy; beat in egg and vanilla. In medium bowl combine flour, baking soda and salt; blend into creamed mixture. Stir in "M&M's"® Semi-Sweet Chocolate Mini Baking Bits and nuts, if using. Drop by heaping tablespoonfuls about 2 inches apart onto ungreased cookie sheets. Bake 9 to 12 minutes or until lightly browned. Cool 1 minute on cookie sheets; cool completely on wire racks. Store in tightly covered container.

Makes about 3 dozen cookies

Hint: *For chewy cookies bake 9 to 10 minutes; for crispy cookies bake 11 to 12 minutes.*

Pan Cookie Variation: *Prepare dough as directed; spread into lightly greased 15×10×1-inch jelly-roll pan. Bake at 375°F for 18 to 22 minutes. Cool completely before cutting into 35 (2-inch) squares. For a more festive look, reserve ½ cup baking bits to sprinkle on top of dough before baking.*

colorific chocolate chip cookies

chocolate crackletops

Your favorite candy colors will peek-a-boo through these cookie pillows.

2 cups all-purpose flour
2 teaspoons baking powder
2 cups granulated sugar
½ cup (1 stick) butter or margarine
4 squares (1 ounce each) unsweetened baking chocolate, chopped
4 large eggs, lightly beaten
2 teaspoons vanilla extract
1¾ cups "M&M's"® Chocolate Mini Baking Bits
   Additional granulated sugar

Combine flour and baking powder; set aside. In 2-quart saucepan over medium heat combine 2 cups sugar, butter and chocolate, stirring until butter and chocolate are melted; remove from heat. Gradually stir in eggs and vanilla. Stir in flour mixture until well blended. Chill mixture 1 hour. Stir in "M&M's"® Chocolate Mini Baking Bits; chill mixture an additional 1 hour.

Preheat oven to 350°F. Line cookie sheets with foil. With sugar-dusted hands, roll dough into 1-inch balls; roll balls in additional granulated sugar. Place about 2 inches apart onto prepared cookie sheets. Bake 10 to 12 minutes. *Do not overbake.* Cool completely on wire racks. Store in tightly covered container.

Makes about 5 dozen cookies

chocolate crackletops

hawaiian drops

Imagine yourself on a tropical island while eating these tasty morsels!

¾ cup (1½ sticks) butter or margarine, softened
¾ cup granulated sugar
¾ cup firmly packed light brown sugar
2 large eggs
1 teaspoon vanilla extract
2 cups quick-cooking or old-fashioned oats, uncooked
1½ cups all-purpose flour
1 teaspoon baking powder
1 teaspoon baking soda
1¾ cups "M&M's"® Chocolate Mini Baking Bits
1 cup shredded coconut
1 cup coarsely chopped macadamia nuts

Preheat oven to 350°F. Cream butter and sugars until light and fluffy; beat in eggs and vanilla. Combine oats, flour, baking powder and baking soda; blend into creamed mixture. Stir in remaining ingredients. Drop by rounded tablespoonfuls onto greased cookie sheets. Bake 13 to 15 minutes.   *Makes about 6 dozen cookies*

jumbles

A cookie chock-full of chocolate, raisins and nuts with just enough dough to hold it all together!

½ cup (1 stick) butter or margarine, softened
½ cup granulated sugar
¼ cup firmly packed light brown sugar
1 large egg
1¼ cups all-purpose flour
½ teaspoon baking soda
1¾ cups "M&M's"® Chocolate Mini Baking Bits
1 cup raisins
1 cup chopped walnuts

Preheat oven to 350°F. Cream butter and sugars until light and fluffy; beat in egg. Combine flour and baking soda; blend into creamed mixture. Stir in remaining ingredients. Drop by rounded tablespoonfuls onto greased cookie sheets. Bake 13 to 15 minutes. Cool 2 to 3 minutes on cookie sheets.   *Makes about 3 dozen cookies*

top to bottom: hawaiian drops and jumbles

11

chocolate raspberry thumbprints

*"M&M's"® Chocolate Mini Baking Bits make these
fun-to-make cookies fun to eat!*

½ cup (1 stick) butter or margarine, softened
½ cup granulated sugar
½ cup firmly packed light brown sugar
 1 large egg
 1 teaspoon vanilla extract
 2 cups all-purpose flour
½ teaspoon baking powder
1¾ cups "M&M's"® Chocolate Mini Baking Bits, divided
    Powdered sugar
½ cup raspberry jam

In large microwave-safe bowl melt butter in microwave; add
sugars and mix well. Stir in egg and vanilla. In medium bowl
combine flour and baking powder; blend into butter mixture. Stir
in *1¼ cups "M&M's"® Chocolate Mini Baking Bits;* refrigerate
dough 1 hour. Preheat oven to 350°F. Lightly grease cookie sheets.
Roll dough into 1-inch balls and place about 2 inches apart onto
prepared cookie sheets. Make an indentation in center of each ball
with thumb. Bake 8 to 10 minutes. Remove from oven and
reindent, if necessary; transfer to wire racks. Lightly dust warm
cookies with powdered sugar; fill each indentation with
½ teaspoon raspberry jam. Sprinkle with remaining *½ cup
"M&M's"® Chocolate Mini Baking Bits.* Cool completely. Dust
with additional powdered sugar, if desired. Store in tightly covered
container.   *Makes about 4 dozen cookies*

13

chocolate raspberry thumbprints

spicy rum corn crisps

Try these crispy treats for a contemporary taste combination.

1 cup (2 sticks) butter or margarine, softened
¾ cup firmly packed light brown sugar
1 teaspoon vanilla extract
½ teaspoon rum extract
1½ cups all-purpose flour
¾ cup yellow cornmeal
1 teaspoon ground ginger
1 teaspoon ground nutmeg
¼ teaspoon ground allspice
¼ teaspoon ground black pepper
1¾ cups "M&M's"® Chocolate Mini Baking Bits, divided

Preheat oven to 350°F. In large bowl cream butter and sugar until light and fluffy. Blend in vanilla and rum extracts. In medium bowl combine flour, cornmeal, ginger, nutmeg, allspice and pepper; stir into creamed mixture just until blended. Stir in *1 cup "M&M's"® Chocolate Mini Baking Bits.* On lightly floured surface, carefully roll dough into 12×8-inch rectangle. Press remaining *¾ cup "M&M's"® Chocolate Mini Baking Bits* into top before cutting into 48 pieces. Transfer to ungreased cookie sheets. Bake 12 to 14 minutes or until lightly browned. Cool completely on wire racks. Store in tightly covered container.

Makes about 4 dozen cookies

15

spicy rum corn crisps

double chocolate walnut drops

These nutty cookies are sure to please any chocolate lover!

¾ cup (1½ sticks) butter or margarine, softened
¾ cup granulated sugar
¾ cup firmly packed light brown sugar
1 large egg
1 teaspoon vanilla extract
2¼ cups all-purpose flour
⅓ cup unsweetened cocoa powder
1 teaspoon baking soda
½ teaspoon salt
1¾ cups "M&M's"® Chocolate Mini Baking Bits
1 cup coarsely chopped English or black walnuts

Preheat oven to 350°F. Lightly grease cookie sheets; set aside. In large bowl cream butter and sugars until light and fluffy; beat in egg and vanilla. In medium bowl combine flour, cocoa powder, baking soda and salt; add to creamed mixture. Stir in "M&M's"® Chocolate Mini Baking Bits and nuts. Drop by heaping tablespoonfuls about 2 inches apart onto prepared cookie sheets. Bake 12 to 14 minutes for chewy cookies or 14 to 16 minutes for crispy cookies. Cool completely on wire racks. Store in tightly covered container. *Makes about 4 dozen cookies*

Variation: *Shape dough into 2-inch-thick roll. Cover with plastic wrap; refrigerate. When ready to bake, slice dough into ¼-inch-thick slices and bake as directed.*

double chocolate walnut drops

colorful sugar cutouts ®

Add colorful fun to your cookies with "M&M's"® Chocolate Mini Baking Bits!

½ **cup (1 stick) butter or margarine**
¼ **cup solid vegetable shortening**
1 **cup granulated sugar**
2 **large eggs**
½ **teaspoon vanilla extract**
2¾ **cups all-purpose flour**
½ **teaspoon baking powder**
¼ **teaspoon baking soda**
¼ **teaspoon salt**
   Vanilla Icing (recipe follows)
   "M&M's"® Chocolate Mini Baking Bits for decoration

In large bowl cream butter, shortening and sugar until light and fluffy; beat in eggs and vanilla. In medium bowl combine flour, baking powder, baking soda and salt; blend into creamed mixture. Wrap and refrigerate dough 2 to 3 hours. Preheat oven to 350°F. Working with half the dough at a time on lightly floured surface, roll to ⅛-inch thickness. Cut into desired shapes using 3-inch cookie cutters. Using rigid spatula carefully transfer to ungreased cookie sheets. Bake 8 to 10 minutes. Cool completely on wire racks. Frost with **Vanilla Icing** and decorate with "M&M's"® Chocolate Mini Baking Bits. Store in tightly covered container.

Makes about 4 dozen cookies

VANILLA ICING: Beat 6 tablespoons butter and 4 cups powdered sugar until well blended; add ½ teaspoon vanilla. Blend in 3 to 4 tablespoons milk, one tablespoon at a time, until of spreading consistency. Divide icing evenly into 3 small bowls. Add red food coloring to one and green to another until mixtures are of desired color. Leave the third portion white.

marbled mocha drops

*The combination of coffee and chocolate gives these
cookies their special flavor.*

1 cup (2 sticks) butter or margarine, softened
⅔ cup granulated sugar
⅔ cup firmly packed light brown sugar
1 large egg
2 tablespoons instant coffee granules, dissolved in
    1 tablespoon water
1 teaspoon vanilla extract
2¼ cups all-purpose flour
1 teaspoon baking soda
½ teaspoon salt
¾ cup coarsely chopped nuts
¼ cup unsweetened cocoa powder
1¾ cups "M&M's"® Semi-Sweet Chocolate Mini Baking Bits

Preheat oven to 350°F. In large bowl cream butter and sugars until
light and fluffy; add egg, dissolved coffee granules and vanilla. In
medium bowl combine flour, baking soda and salt. Blend flour
mixture and nuts into creamed mixture. Remove half of the dough
to small bowl; set aside. Blend cocoa powder into remaining
dough. Stir in "M&M's"® Semi-Sweet Chocolate Mini Baking Bits
into the two doughs, using half for each. Combine two doughs by
folding together just enough to marble, about 4 strokes. Drop by
heaping tablespoonfuls about 2 inches apart onto ungreased
cookie sheets. Bake 10 to 12 minutes or just until set. *Do not
overbake.* Cool 1 minute on cookie sheets; cool completely on wire
racks. Store in tightly covered container.

Makes about 2½ dozen cookies

patchwork cream cheese cookies

A patchwork of color enhances a delicate taste!

½ cup (1 stick) butter or margarine, softened
3 ounces cream cheese, softened
½ cup granulated sugar
1 large egg
1 teaspoon grated orange zest
1 teaspoon vanilla extract
2 cups all-purpose flour
½ teaspoon baking soda
1¾ cups "M&M's"® Chocolate Mini Baking Bits
Granulated sugar

Preheat oven to 350°F. Cream butter, cream cheese and sugar until light and fluffy; add egg, orange zest and vanilla. Combine flour and baking soda; blend into creamed mixture. Stir in baking bits. Shape dough into 1-inch balls; place about 2 inches apart onto greased cookie sheets. Gently flatten cookies with bottom of greased glass dipped in sugar. Bake 12 to 15 minutes.

Makes about 3 dozen cookies

eggnog crisps

These crispy treats will become a year-round favorite!

½ cup (1 stick) butter or margarine, melted
1 cup granulated sugar
1 large egg
1½ teaspoons brandy extract
1½ cups cake flour
½ cup ground pecans
½ teaspoon ground nutmeg
1¾ cups "M&M's"® Chocolate Mini Baking Bits
36 pecan halves

Preheat oven to 375°F. Cream butter and sugar until light and fluffy; add egg and brandy extract. Combine flour, ground pecans and nutmeg; blend into creamed mixture. Stir in baking bits. Drop by heaping tablespoonfuls onto greased cookie sheets; top each with 1 pecan half. Bake 10 to 11 minutes or until edges turn light golden. Cool 1 minute on cookie sheets. *Makes about 3 dozen cookies*

*left to right: patchwork cream cheese
cookies and eggnog crisps*

crispy oat drops

A crispy cookie favorite for the cookie jar.

1 cup (2 sticks) butter or margarine, softened
½ cup granulated sugar
½ cup firmly packed light brown sugar
1 large egg
2 cups all-purpose flour
½ cup quick-cooking or old-fashioned oats, uncooked
1 teaspoon cream of tartar
½ teaspoon baking soda
¼ teaspoon salt
1¾ cups "M&M's"® Semi-Sweet Chocolate Mini Baking Bits
1 cup toasted rice cereal
½ cup shredded coconut
½ cup coarsely chopped pecans

Preheat oven to 350°F. In large bowl cream butter and sugars until light and fluffy; beat in egg. In medium bowl combine flour, oats, cream of tartar, baking soda and salt; blend flour mixture into creamed mixture. Stir in "M&M's"® Semi-Sweet Chocolate Mini Baking Bits, cereal, coconut and pecans. Drop by heaping tablespoonfuls about 2 inches apart onto ungreased cookie sheets. Bake 10 to 13 minutes or until lightly browned. Cool completely on wire racks. Store in tightly covered container.

Makes about 4 dozen cookies

crispy oat drops

chocolate molasses gems

Molasses gives these "gems" their soft and chewy texture.

¾ cup butter-flavored solid vegetable shortening
1 cup firmly packed dark brown sugar
1 large egg
⅓ cup molasses
2½ cups all-purpose flour
2 teaspoons baking soda
1 teaspoon ground cinnamon
1 teaspoon ground ginger
¼ teaspoon salt
¼ teaspoon ground cloves
1¾ cups "M&M's"® Chocolate Mini Baking Bits
Granulated sugar

Preheat oven to 350°F. In large bowl cream shortening and sugar until light and fluffy; beat in egg and molasses. In medium bowl combine flour, baking soda, cinnamon, ginger, salt and cloves; blend into creamed mixture. Stir in "M&M's"® Chocolate Mini Baking Bits. Shape dough into 1½-inch balls; roll in granulated sugar. Place about 2 inches apart onto ungreased cookie sheets. Bake 8 to 10 minutes or until set. *Do not overbake.* Cool 1 minute on cookie sheets; cool completely on wire racks. Store in tightly covered container. *Makes about 3 dozen cookies*

chewy milk chocolate oatmeal cookies

"M&M's"® Milk Chocolate Mini Baking Bits add excitement to this traditional taste in cookies!

1¼ cups (2½ sticks) butter or margarine, softened
¾ cup firmly packed light brown sugar
½ cup granulated sugar
1 large egg
1½ teaspoons vanilla extract
3 cups quick-cooking or old-fashioned oats, uncooked
1½ cups all-purpose flour
1 teaspoon baking soda
1 teaspoon salt
1¾ cups "M&M's"® Milk Chocolate Mini Baking Bits

Preheat oven to 375°F. In large bowl cream butter and sugars until light and fluffy; beat in egg and vanilla. In medium bowl combine oats, flour, baking soda and salt; blend into creamed mixture. Stir in "M&M's"® Milk Chocolate Mini Baking Bits. Drop by rounded tablespoonfuls about 2 inches apart onto ungreased cookie sheets. Bake 8 to 9 minutes or until set. *Do not overbake.* Cool 1 minute on cookie sheets; cool completely on wire racks. Store in tightly covered container.   *Makes about 4 dozen cookies*

spicy lemon crescents

Cinnamon, cardamom and nutmeg give these cookies their special flavor.

1 cup (2 sticks) butter or margarine, softened
1½ cups powdered sugar, divided
½ teaspoon lemon extract
½ teaspoon grated lemon zest
2 cups cake flour
½ cup finely chopped almonds, walnuts or pecans
1 teaspoon ground cinnamon
½ teaspoon ground cardamom
½ teaspoon ground nutmeg
1¾ cups "M&M's"® Chocolate Mini Baking Bits

Preheat oven to 375°F. Lightly grease cookie sheets; set aside. In large bowl cream butter and *½ cup sugar;* add lemon extract and zest until well blended. In medium bowl combine flour, nuts, cinnamon, cardamom and nutmeg; add to creamed mixture until well blended. Stir in "M&M's"® Chocolate Mini Baking Bits. Using 1 tablespoon of dough at a time, form into crescent shapes; place about 2 inches apart onto prepared cookie sheets. Bake 12 to 14 minutes or until edges are golden. Cool 2 minutes on cookie sheets. Gently roll warm crescents in remaining *1 cup sugar.* Cool completely on wire racks. Store in tightly covered container.

Makes about 2 dozen cookies

spicy lemon crescents

chocolate banana walnut drops

A colorful twist on a favorite flavor combination!

½ cup (1 stick) butter or margarine, softened
½ cup solid vegetable shortening
1¼ cups firmly packed light brown sugar
1 large egg
1 medium banana, mashed (about ½ cup)
2¼ cups all-purpose flour
1 teaspoon baking soda
1 teaspoon ground cinnamon
½ teaspoon ground nutmeg
¼ teaspoon salt
2 cups quick-cooking or old-fashioned oats, uncooked
1 cup coarsely chopped walnuts
1¾ cups "M&M's"® Chocolate Mini Baking Bits

Preheat oven to 350°F. In large bowl cream butter, shortening and sugar until light and fluffy; beat in egg and banana. In medium bowl combine flour, baking soda, cinnamon, nutmeg and salt; blend into creamed mixture. Blend in oats and nuts. Stir in "M&M's"® Chocolate Mini Baking Bits. Drop by tablespoonfuls about 2 inches apart onto ungreased cookie sheets. Bake 8 to 10 minutes just until set. *Do not overbake.* Cool 1 minute on cookie sheets; cool completely on wire racks. Store in tightly covered container. *Makes about 3 dozen cookies*

chocolate banana walnut drops

brownies & bars

double-decker confetti brownies

Two favorite cookie bar tastes in one!

¾ cup (1½ sticks) butter or margarine, softened
1 cup granulated sugar
1 cup firmly packed light brown sugar
3 large eggs
1 teaspoon vanilla extract
2½ cups all-purpose flour, divided
2½ teaspoons baking powder
½ teaspoon salt
⅓ cup unsweetened cocoa powder
1 tablespoon butter or margarine, melted
1 cup "M&M's"® Semi-Sweet Chocolate Mini Baking Bits, divided

Preheat oven to 350°F. Lightly grease 13×9×2-inch baking pan; set aside. In large bowl cream butter and sugars until light and fluffy; beat in eggs and vanilla. In medium bowl combine **2¼ cups flour,** baking powder and salt; blend into creamed mixture. Divide batter in half. Blend together cocoa powder and melted butter; stir into one half of the dough. Spread cocoa dough evenly into prepared baking pan. Stir remaining ¼ **cup flour** and ½ **cup "M&M's"®** **Semi-Sweet Chocolate Mini Baking Bits** into remaining dough; spread evenly over cocoa dough in pan. Sprinkle with remaining ½ **cup "M&M's"® Semi-Sweet Chocolate Mini Baking Bits.** Bake 25 to 30 minutes or until edges start to pull away from sides of pan. Cool completely. Cut into bars. Store in tightly covered container. *Makes 24 brownies*

double-decker confetti brownies

oasis date bars

Dates and coconut make these bars moist and chewy.

  $^1\!/_2$ cup (1 stick) butter or margarine, softened
  $^3\!/_4$ cup firmly packed light brown sugar
   2 large eggs
   2 teaspoons vanilla extract
  $1^1\!/_2$ cups all-purpose flour
  $^1\!/_2$ cup shredded coconut
   1 teaspoon baking powder
  $1^3\!/_4$ cups "M&M's"® Chocolate Mini Baking Bits, divided
   1 cup chopped pitted dates
  $^1\!/_2$ cup chopped almonds
     Lemon Glaze (recipe follows)

Preheat oven to 350°F. Lightly grease 13×9×2-inch baking pan; set aside. In large bowl cream butter and sugar until light and fluffy; beat in eggs and vanilla. In separate bowl combine flour, coconut and baking powder; blend into creamed mixture. Stir in *$1^1\!/_4$ cups "M&M's"® Chocolate Mini Baking Bits,* dates and nuts. *Dough will be stiff.* Spread into prepared pan; sprinkle with remaining *$^1\!/_2$ cup "M&M's"® Chocolate Mini Baking Bits.* Bake 35 to 40 minutes or until toothpick inserted in center comes out clean. Cool completely; drizzle with **Lemon Glaze.** Cut into bars. Store in tightly covered container. *Makes 24 bars*

LEMON GLAZE: Combine 1 cup powdered sugar, 2 tablespoons lemon juice and 1 tablespoon grated lemon zest until smooth. Place in resealable plastic sandwich bag; seal bag. Cut a tiny piece off one corner of the bag (not more than $^1\!/_8$ inch). Drizzle glaze over bars.

Variation: For thicker bars, pour mixture into lightly greased 8×8×2-inch baking pan; bake 40 to 45 minutes. Reduce Lemon Glaze ingredients by half. Makes 16 bars.

oasis date bars

minty shortbread squares

Chocolate and mint are perfect companions for these colorful squares.

1½ **cups (3 sticks) butter, softened**
1½ **cups powdered sugar**
 2 **teaspoons mint extract, divided**
 3 **cups all-purpose flour**
 ½ **cup unsweetened cocoa powder**
1¾ **cups "M&M's"® Chocolate Mini Baking Bits, divided**
 1 **16-ounce container prepared white frosting**
 Several drops green food coloring

Preheat oven to 325°F. Lightly grease 15×10×1-inch baking pan; set aside. In large bowl cream butter and sugar until light and fluffy; add *1 teaspoon mint extract.* In medium bowl combine flour and cocoa powder; blend into creamed mixture. Stir in *1 cup "M&M's"® Chocolate Mini Baking Bits. Dough will be stiff.* Press dough into prepared baking pan with lightly floured fingers. Bake 16 to 18 minutes. Cool completely. Combine frosting, remaining *1 teaspoon mint extract* and green food coloring. Spread frosting over shortbread; sprinkle with remaining *¾ cup "M&M's"® Chocolate Mini Baking Bits.* Cut into squares. Store in tightly covered container. *Makes 36 squares*

Variation: Use 1 (19- to 21-ounce) package fudge brownie mix, prepared according to package directions for chewy brownies, adding 1 teaspoon mint extract to liquid ingredients. Stir in 1 cup "M&M's"® Chocolate Mini Baking Bits. Spread dough in lightly greased 13×9×2-inch baking pan. Bake in preheated oven according to package directions. Cool completely. Prepare frosting and decorate as directed above. Store in tightly covered container. Makes 24 squares.

minty shortbread squares

chocolate marbled blondies

*Savor two great tastes—delicious chocolate cheesecake
swirled into moist, chewy blondies!*

½ cup (1 stick) butter or margarine, softened
½ cup firmly packed light brown sugar
1 large egg
2 teaspoons vanilla extract
1½ cups all-purpose flour
1¼ teaspoons baking soda
1 cup "M&M's"® Chocolate Mini Baking Bits, divided
4 ounces cream cheese, softened
2 tablespoons granulated sugar
1 large egg yolk
¼ cup unsweetened cocoa powder

Preheat oven to 350°F. Lightly grease 9×9×2-inch baking pan; set
aside. In large bowl cream butter and brown sugar until light and
fluffy; beat in egg and vanilla. In medium bowl combine flour and
baking soda; blend into creamed mixture. Stir in ⅔ *cup "M&M's"®
Chocolate Mini Baking Bits;* set aside. *Dough will be stiff.* In
separate bowl beat together cream cheese, granulated sugar and
egg yolk until smooth; stir in cocoa powder until well blended.
Place chocolate-cheese mixture in six equal portions evenly onto
bottom of prepared pan. Place reserved dough around cheese
mixture and swirl slightly with tines of fork. Pat down evenly on
top. Sprinkle with remaining ⅓ *cup "M&M's"® Chocolate Mini
Baking Bits.* Bake 25 to 30 minutes until toothpick inserted in
center comes out with moist crumbs. Cool completely. Cut into
bars. Store in refrigerator in tightly covered container.

Makes 16 bars

chocolate marbled blondies

colorful caramel bites

Creamy caramel and chocolate give these bars their rich taste!

1 cup plus 6 tablespoons all-purpose flour, divided
1 cup quick-cooking or old-fashioned oats, uncooked
¾ cup firmly packed light brown sugar
½ teaspoon baking soda
¼ teaspoon salt
¾ cup (1½ sticks) butter or margarine, melted
1¾ cups "M&M's"® Chocolate Mini Baking Bits, divided
1½ cups chopped pecans, divided
1 jar (12 ounces) caramel ice cream topping

Preheat oven to 350°F. Combine *1 cup flour,* oats, sugar, baking soda and salt; blend in melted butter to form crumbly mixture. Press half the crumb mixture onto bottom of 9×9×2-inch baking pan; bake 10 minutes. Sprinkle with *1 cup baking bits* and *1 cup nuts.* Blend remaining *6 tablespoons flour* with caramel topping; pour over top. Combine remaining crumb mixture, remaining ¾ *cup baking bits* and remaining ½ *cup nuts;* sprinkle over caramel layer. Bake 20 to 25 minutes or until golden brown.

Makes 36 bars

chocolate oat shortbread

A delightful change to a traditional bar!

1 cup (2 sticks) butter, softened
1 cup powdered sugar
2 teaspoons vanilla extract
1½ cups all-purpose flour
1 cup quick-cooking or old-fashioned oats, uncooked
¼ cup unsweetened cocoa powder
1 teaspoon ground cinnamon
1¾ cups "M&M's"® Chocolate Mini Baking Bits, divided

Preheat oven to 325°F. Lightly grease 13×9×2-inch pan. Cream butter and sugar until light and fluffy; add vanilla. Combine flour, oats, cocoa powder and cinnamon; blend into creamed mixture. Stir in *1 cup baking bits;* press dough into prepared pan. Sprinkle remaining ¾ *cup baking bits* over dough; press in lightly. Bake 20 to 25 minutes or until set. *Makes 36 to 48 bars*

39

*top to bottom: colorful caramel bites
and chocolate oat shortbread*

chocolate orange gems

These moist, chewy bars sure are a delight to eat!

⅔ cup butter-flavored solid vegetable shortening
¾ cup firmly packed light brown sugar
1 large egg
¼ cup orange juice
1 tablespoon grated orange zest
2¼ cups all-purpose flour
½ teaspoon baking powder
½ teaspoon baking soda
½ teaspoon salt
1¾ cups "M&M's"® Chocolate Mini Baking Bits
1 cup coarsely chopped pecans
⅓ cup orange marmalade
Vanilla Glaze (recipe follows)

Preheat oven to 350°F. In large bowl cream shortening and sugar until light and fluffy; beat in egg, orange juice and orange zest. In medium bowl combine flour, baking powder, baking soda and salt; blend into creamed mixture. Stir in "M&M's"® Chocolate Mini Baking Bits and nuts. Reserve 1 cup dough; spread remaining dough into ungreased 13×9×2-inch baking pan. Spread marmalade evenly over top of dough to within ½ inch of edges. Drop reserved dough by teaspoonfuls randomly over marmalade. Bake 25 to 30 minutes or until light golden brown. *Do not overbake.* Cool completely; drizzle with **Vanilla Glaze.** Cut into bars. Store in tightly covered container. *Makes 24 bars*

VANILLA GLAZE: Combine 1 cup powdered sugar and 1 to 1½ tablespoons warm water until desired consistency. Place glaze in resealable plastic sandwich bag; seal bag. Cut a tiny piece off one corner of the bag (not more than ⅛ inch). Drizzle glaze over cookies.

chocolate orange gems

chocolate cream cheese squares

These smooth and creamy squares are sure to delight all dessert lovers!

¾ cup (1½ sticks) butter or margarine, softened
¾ cup powdered sugar
1¾ cups all-purpose flour, divided
⅔ cup finely chopped pecans, divided
¼ cup cocoa powder
1 8-ounce package cream cheese, softened
1 large egg
1 14-ounce can sweetened condensed milk
1 teaspoon vanilla extract
1 cup "M&M's"® Semi-Sweet Chocolate Mini Baking Bits

Preheat oven to 350°F. Cream butter and sugar until light and fluffy. Combine *1½ cups flour, ⅓ cup nuts* and cocoa powder; blend into creamed mixture. *Do not overbeat.* Press two-thirds of mixture onto bottom of ungreased 13×9×2-inch baking pan; bake 10 minutes. Beat cream cheese and egg until light and fluffy. Slowly add condensed milk and vanilla; mix until smooth. Pour over crust. Add remaining *¼ cup flour* to remaining crust mixture until crumbly; sprinkle over cheese mixture. Combine remaining *⅓ cup nuts* and "M&M's"® Semi-Sweet Chocolate Mini Baking Bits; press lightly into cream cheese layer. Bake 30 to 40 minutes until set. Cool; cut into 2-inch squares. Store in refrigerator.

Makes 24 squares

chocolate berry squares

Luscious jam is the "berry" special ingredient in these moist, delicious squares.

1 cup (2 sticks) butter or margarine, softened
½ cup granulated sugar
½ cup firmly packed light brown sugar
1 large egg
1 teaspoon vanilla extract
2 cups all-purpose flour
¾ teaspoon baking soda
¾ teaspoon salt
1¾ cups "M&M's"® Semi-Sweet Chocolate Mini Baking Bits
½ cup seedless red raspberry jam

Preheat oven to 350°F. Line 13×9×2-inch baking pan with aluminum foil, extending it 1 inch beyond each end of pan; set aside. In large bowl cream butter and sugars until light and fluffy; beat in egg and vanilla. In medium bowl combine flour, baking soda and salt; blend into creamed mixture. Stir in "M&M's"® Semi-Sweet Chocolate Mini Baking Bits. Reserve 1 cup dough. Spread remaining dough into prepared pan. Spread jam evenly over top of dough to within ½ inch of edges. Drop reserved dough by teaspoonfuls randomly over jam. Bake 30 to 35 minutes or until light golden brown. Cool completely in pan. Remove by lifting foil. Cut into squares. Store in tightly covered container.

Makes 24 squares

chewy chocolate granola treats

Treat yourself to these crunchy, chewy delights!

¼ cup (½ stick) butter or margarine, softened
¼ cup solid vegetable shortening
1 cup firmly packed light brown sugar
1 large egg
1½ teaspoons vanilla extract
1 cup all-purpose flour
½ teaspoon baking soda
¼ teaspoon salt
½ teaspoon ground cinnamon
¼ cup milk
2 cups granola cereal
1¾ cups "M&M's"® Semi-Sweet Chocolate Mini Baking Bits, divided
1 cup shredded coconut

Preheat oven to 350°F. Grease 15×10×1-inch baking pan; set aside. In large bowl cream butter, shortening, sugar, egg and vanilla. In medium bowl combine flour, baking soda, salt and cinnamon; blend into creamed mixture alternately with milk. Stir in cereal, *1¼ cups "M&M's"® Semi-Sweet Chocolate Mini Baking Bits* and coconut. Spread mixture into prepared pan; sprinkle with remaining *½ cup "M&M's"® Semi-Sweet Chocolate Mini Baking Bits* and press in lightly. Bake 25 to 30 minutes until golden. Cool completely. Cut into bars. Store in tightly covered container.

Makes 48 bars

marvelous cookie bars

A wonderful way to combine the great tastes of chocolate and cherries in these chewy, gooey bars!

½ cup (1 stick) butter or margarine, softened
1 cup firmly packed light brown sugar
2 large eggs
1⅓ cups all-purpose flour
1 cup quick-cooking or old-fashioned oats, uncooked
⅓ cup unsweetened cocoa powder
1 teaspoon baking powder
½ teaspoon salt
¼ teaspoon baking soda
½ cup chopped walnuts, divided
1 cup "M&M's"® Semi-Sweet Chocolate Mini Baking Bits, divided
½ cup cherry preserves
¼ cup shredded coconut

Preheat oven to 350°F. Lightly grease 9×9×2-inch baking pan; set aside. In large bowl cream butter and sugar until light and fluffy; beat in eggs. In medium bowl combine flour, oats, cocoa powder, baking powder, salt and baking soda; blend into creamed mixture. Stir in *¼ cup nuts* and ¾ *cup "M&M's"® Semi-Sweet Chocolate Mini Baking Bits.* Reserve 1 cup dough; spread remaining dough into prepared pan. Combine preserves, coconut and remaining *¼ cup nuts;* spread evenly over dough to within ½ inch of edge. Drop reserved dough by rounded teaspoonfuls over preserves mixture; sprinkle with remaining *¼ cup "M&M's"® Semi-Sweet Chocolate Mini Baking Bits.* Bake 25 to 30 minutes or until slightly firm near edges. Cool completely. Cut into bars. Store in tightly covered container. *Makes 16 bars*

marvelous cookie bars

double chocolate fantasy bars

*Double chocolate makes these cookie bars
divinely delectable!*

2 cups chocolate cookie crumbs
⅓ cup (5⅓ tablespoons) butter or margarine, melted
1 14-ounce can sweetened condensed milk
1¾ cups "M&M's"® Semi-Sweet Chocolate Mini Baking Bits
1 cup shredded coconut
1 cup chopped walnuts or pecans

Preheat oven to 350°F. In large bowl combine cookie crumbs and butter; press mixture onto bottom of 13×9×2-inch baking pan. Pour condensed milk evenly over crumbs. Combine "M&M's"® Semi-Sweet Chocolate Mini Baking Bits, coconut and nuts. Sprinkle mixture evenly over condensed milk; press down lightly. Bake 25 to 30 minutes or until set. Cool completely. Cut into bars. Store in tightly covered container. *Makes 32 bars*

rainbow blondies

A delicious way to brighten your day!

1 cup (2 sticks) butter or margarine, softened
1½ cups firmly packed light brown sugar
1 large egg
1 teaspoon vanilla extract
2 cups all-purpose flour
½ teaspoon baking soda
1¾ cups "M&M's"® Semi-Sweet or Milk Chocolate Mini Baking Bits
1 cup chopped walnuts or pecans

Preheat oven to 350°F. Lightly grease 13×9×2-inch baking pan; set aside. In large bowl cream butter and sugar until light and fluffy; beat in egg and vanilla. In medium bowl combine flour and baking soda; add to creamed mixture just until combined. *Dough will be stiff.* Stir in "M&M's"® Chocolate Mini Baking Bits and nuts. Spread dough into prepared baking pan. Bake 30 to 35 minutes or until toothpick inserted in center comes out with moist crumbs. *Do not overbake.* Cool completely. Cut into bars. Store in tightly covered container. *Makes 24 bars*

47

left to right: double chocolate fantasy bars and rainbow blondies

coconut pecan bars

If you like pecan pie, you'll love these layered cookie bars!

1¼ cups granulated sugar, divided
½ cup plus 3 tablespoons all-purpose flour, divided
1½ cups finely chopped pecans, divided
¾ cup (1½ sticks) butter or margarine, softened, divided
2 large eggs
1 tablespoon vanilla extract
1¾ cups "M&M's"® Chocolate Mini Baking Bits, divided
1 cup shredded coconut

Preheat oven to 350°F. Lightly grease 13×9×2-inch baking pan; set aside. In large bowl combine ¾ *cup sugar, ½ cup flour* and *½ cup nuts;* add ¼ *cup melted butter* and mix well. Press mixture onto bottom of prepared pan. Bake 10 minutes or until set; cool slightly. In large bowl cream remaining ½ *cup butter* and ½ *cup sugar;* beat in eggs and vanilla. Combine *1 cup "M&M's"® Chocolate Mini Baking Bits* and remaining *3 tablespoons flour;* stir into creamed mixture. Spread mixture over cooled crust. Combine coconut and remaining *1 cup nuts;* sprinkle over batter. Sprinkle remaining ¾ *cup "M&M's"® Chocolate Mini Baking Bits* over coconut and nuts; pat down lightly. Bake 25 to 30 minutes or until set. Cool completely. Cut into bars. Store in tightly covered container.   *Makes 24 bars*

coconut pecan bars

oatmeal chocolate cherry bars

Try these chewy squares for the luscious taste of chocolate and cherries.

½ cup (1 stick) butter or margarine, softened
¼ cup solid vegetable shortening
1 cup firmly packed light brown sugar
1 large egg
1 teaspoon vanilla extract
2½ cups quick-cooking or old-fashioned oats, uncooked
1 cup all-purpose flour
1 teaspoon baking soda
1¾ cups "M&M's"® Chocolate Mini Baking Bits, divided
1 cup dried cherries, plumped*

Preheat oven to 350°F. Lightly grease 13×9×2-inch baking pan; set aside. In large bowl cream butter and shortening until light and fluffy; beat in sugar, egg and vanilla. In medium bowl combine oats, flour and baking soda; blend into creamed mixture. Stir in *1¼ cups "M&M's"® Chocolate Mini Baking Bits* and cherries. Spread batter evenly in prepared pan; top with remaining *½ cup "M&M's"® Chocolate Mini Baking Bits.* Bake 25 to 30 minutes or until toothpick inserted in center comes out clean. Cool completely. Cut into squares. Store in tightly covered container.

Makes 24 bars

*To plump cherries, pour 1½ cups boiling water over cherries and let stand 10 minutes. Drain well and use as directed above.

Variation: *To make cookies, drop dough by rounded tablespoonfuls about 2 inches apart onto lightly greased cookie sheets; place 4 to 5 pieces of remaining ½ cup "M&M's"® Chocolate Mini Baking Bits on top of each cookie. Bake 13 to 15 minutes. Cool 2 to 3 minutes on cookie sheets; remove to wire racks to cool completely. Store in tightly covered container. Makes about 4 dozen cookies.*

oatmeal chocolate cherry bars

celebrations & special occasions

color-bright ice cream sandwiches

*Delight family and friends with these make-ahead treats—
a perfect end to a summer barbecue.*

¾ cup (1½ sticks) butter or margarine, softened
¾ cup creamy peanut butter
1¼ cups firmly packed light brown sugar
1 large egg
1 teaspoon vanilla extract
1½ cups all-purpose flour
1 teaspoon baking soda
¼ teaspoon salt
1¾ cups "M&M's"® Chocolate Mini Baking Bits, divided
2 quarts vanilla or chocolate ice cream, slightly softened

Preheat oven to 350°F. In large bowl cream butter, peanut butter
and sugar until light and fluffy; beat in egg and vanilla. In medium
bowl combine flour, baking soda and salt; blend into creamed
mixture. Stir in *1⅓ cups "M&M's"® Chocolate Mini Baking Bits.*
Shape dough into 1¼-inch balls. Place about 2 inches apart on
ungreased cookie sheets. Gently flatten to about ½-inch thickness
with fingertips. Place 7 or 8 of the remaining *"M&M's"® Chocolate
Mini Baking Bits* on each cookie; press in lightly. Bake 10 to
12 minutes or until edges are light brown. *Do not overbake.* Cool
about 1 minute on cookie sheets; cool completely on wire racks.
Assemble cookies in pairs with about ⅓ cup ice cream; press
cookies together lightly. Wrap each sandwich in plastic wrap;
freeze until firm.   *Makes about 24 ice cream sandwiches*

color-bright ice cream sandwiches

chocolate macadamia chewies

A taste of the tropics without leaving your kitchen!

¾ cup (1½ sticks) butter or margarine, softened
⅔ cup firmly packed light brown sugar
1 large egg
1 teaspoon vanilla extract
1¾ cups all-purpose flour
¾ teaspoon baking soda
¼ teaspoon salt
¾ cup (3½ ounces) coarsely chopped macadamia nuts
½ cup shredded coconut
1¾ cups "M&M's"® Chocolate Mini Baking Bits

Preheat oven to 350°F. In large bowl cream butter and sugar until light and fluffy; beat in egg and vanilla. In medium bowl combine flour, baking soda and salt; blend into creamed mixture. Blend in nuts and coconut. Stir in "M&M's"® Chocolate Mini Baking Bits. Drop by heaping teaspoonfuls about 2 inches apart onto ungreased cookie sheets; flatten slightly with back of spoon. Bake 8 to 10 minutes or until set. *Do not overbake.* Cool 1 minute on cookie sheets; cool completely on wire racks. Store in tightly covered container. *Makes about 4 dozen cookies*

chocolate macadamia chewies

marbled biscotti

It's a tradition to dunk these crunchy, dried cookie slices into coffee or milk!

½ cup (1 stick) butter or margarine, softened
1 cup granulated sugar
2 large eggs
1 teaspoon vanilla extract
2½ cups all-purpose flour
1 teaspoon baking powder
1 teaspoon baking soda
1¾ cups "M&M's"® Chocolate Mini Baking Bits, divided
1 cup slivered almonds, toasted*
¼ cup unsweetened cocoa powder
2 tablespoons instant coffee granules

Preheat oven to 350°F. Lightly grease cookie sheets; set aside. In large bowl cream butter and sugar until light and fluffy; beat in eggs and vanilla. In medium bowl combine flour, baking powder and baking soda; blend into creamed mixture. *Dough will be stiff.* Stir in *1¼ cups "M&M's"® Chocolate Mini Baking Bits* and nuts. Divide dough in half. Add cocoa powder and coffee granules to one half of the dough, mixing to blend. On well-floured surface, gently knead doughs together just enough to marble. Divide dough in half and gently roll each half into 12×2-inch log; place on prepared cookie sheets at least 4 inches apart. Press remaining *½ cup "M&M's"® Chocolate Mini Baking Bits* onto outside of both logs. Bake 25 minutes. *Dough will spread.* Cool logs 15 to 20 minutes. Slice each log into 12 slices; arrange on cookie sheet cut-side down. Bake an additional 10 minutes. (For softer biscotti, omit second baking.) Cool completely. Store in tightly covered container. *Makes 24 pieces*

To toast almonds, spread in single layer on baking sheet. Bake at 350°F for 7 to 10 minutes until light golden, stirring occasionally. Remove almonds from pan and cool completely before using.

marbled biscotti

cranberry cheese bars

No need to wait for a special occasion to enjoy these chocolatey, fruity cheesecake bars!

2 cups all-purpose flour
1½ cups quick-cooking or old-fashioned oats, uncooked
¾ cup plus 1 tablespoon firmly packed light brown sugar, divided
1 cup (2 sticks) butter or margarine, softened
1¾ cups "M&M's"® Chocolate Mini Baking Bits, divided
1 8-ounce package cream cheese
1 14-ounce can sweetened condensed milk
¼ cup lemon juice
1 teaspoon vanilla extract
2 tablespoons cornstarch
1 16-ounce can whole berry cranberry sauce

Preheat oven to 350°F. Lightly grease 13×9×2-inch baking pan; set aside. In large bowl combine flour, oats, ¾ *cup sugar* and butter; mix until crumbly. Reserve 1½ cups crumb mixture for topping. Stir ½ *cup "M&M's"® Chocolate Mini Baking Bits* into remaining crumb mixture; press into prepared pan. Bake 15 minutes. Cool completely. In large bowl beat cream cheese until light and fluffy; gradually mix in condensed milk, lemon juice and vanilla until smooth. Pour evenly over crust. In small bowl combine remaining *1 tablespoon sugar,* cornstarch and cranberry sauce. Spoon over cream cheese mixture. Stir remaining *1¼ cups "M&M's"® Chocolate Mini Baking Bits* into reserved crumb mixture. Sprinkle over cranberry mixture. Bake 40 minutes. Cool at room temperature; refrigerate before cutting. Store in refrigerator in tightly covered container. *Makes 32 bars*

cranberry cheese bars

festive rugelach

A colorful rendition of a traditional recipe!

1½ cups (3 sticks) butter or margarine, softened
12 ounces cream cheese, softened
3½ cups all-purpose flour, divided
½ cup powdered sugar
¾ cup granulated sugar
1½ teaspoons ground cinnamon
1¾ cups "M&M's"® Chocolate Mini Baking Bits, divided
    Powdered sugar

Preheat oven to 350°F. Lightly grease cookie sheets; set aside. In large bowl cream butter and cream cheese. Slowly work in *3 cups flour.* Divide dough into 6 equal pieces and shape into squares. Lightly flour dough, wrap in waxed paper and refrigerate at least 1 hour. Combine remaining *½ cup flour* and ½ cup powdered sugar. Remove one piece of dough at a time from refrigerator; roll out on surface dusted with flour-sugar mixture to 18×5×⅛-inch-thick strip. Combine granulated sugar and cinnamon. Sprinkle dough strip with 2 tablespoons cinnamon-sugar mixture. Sprinkle about *¼ cup "M&M's"® Chocolate Mini Baking Bits* on wide end of each strip. Roll dough starting at wide end to completely enclose baking bits. Cut strip into 1½-inch lengths; place seam-side down about 2 inches apart onto prepared cookie sheets. Repeat with remaining ingredients. Bake 16 to 18 minutes or until golden. Cool completely on wire racks. Sprinkle with powdered sugar. Store in tightly covered container.

Makes about 6 dozen cookies

Variation: For crescent shapes, roll each piece of dough into 12-inch circle. Sprinkle with cinnamon-sugar mixture. Cut into 12 wedges. Place about ½ teaspoon "M&M's"® Chocolate Mini Baking Bits at wide end of each wedge and roll up to enclose baking bits. Place seam-side down on prepared baking sheet and proceed as directed above.

festive rugelach

giant easter egg cookies

Add these "eggs" to any basket for a special spring treat!

  2 cups (4 sticks) butter or margarine, softened
  ½ cup granulated sugar
  ½ cup firmly packed light brown sugar
  1 large egg
  1 teaspoon vanilla extract
  3½ cups all-purpose flour
  ½ teaspoon salt
  1 cup chopped pecans
  1¾ cups "M&M's"® Semi-Sweet Chocolate Mini Baking Bits,
      divided
    Decorating icing in tubes

Preheat oven to 375°F. In large bowl cream butter and sugars until light and fluffy; beat in egg and vanilla. In medium bowl combine flour and salt; blend into creamed mixture. Stir in nuts and *1¼ cups "M&M's"® Semi-Sweet Chocolate Mini Baking Bits.* Drop by ¼ cupfuls about 4 inches apart onto lightly greased cookie sheets; flatten each into an egg shape about 4×2¾ inches. Bake 11 to 13 minutes or until lightly browned. Carefully remove to wire racks to cool completely. Decorate with icing and remaining *½ cup "M&M's"® Semi-Sweet Chocolate Mini Baking Bits.* Store in tightly covered container.

Makes about 2½ dozen cookies

fanciful party mix

Quick to make and easy to nibble, this party mix is sure to be a favorite!

  1¾ cups "M&M's"® Chocolate Mini Baking Bits
  1 cup banana chips, coarsely broken
  1 cup honey roasted peanuts
  1 cup raisins

Combine all ingredients until well blended. Store in tightly covered container.

Makes about 5 cups

rainbow streusel coffee cake

Make your next coffee break or brunch more festive with this tasty cake.

¾ cup (1½ sticks) butter or margarine, divided
1 cup granulated sugar
2 large eggs
1 teaspoon vanilla extract
2½ cups all-purpose flour, divided
1 teaspoon baking powder
1¾ cups "M&M's"® Chocolate Mini Baking Bits, divided
4 KUDOS® Milk Chocolate Granola Bars Peanut Butter, chopped
½ cup firmly packed light brown sugar

Preheat oven to 350°F. Grease 9-inch springform pan. In large bowl cream *½ cup butter* and granulated sugar until light and fluffy; beat in eggs and vanilla. In medium bowl combine *2 cups flour* and baking powder; blend into creamed mixture. *Do not overmix.* Stir in *¾ cup "M&M's"® Chocolate Mini Baking Bits.* Spread batter into prepared pan. In separate bowl combine chopped KUDOS®, remaining *½ cup flour*, brown sugar and *¼ cup melted butter* to create streusel. Add remaining *1 cup "M&M's"® Chocolate Mini Baking Bits* and toss to mix. Sprinkle streusel evenly over batter. Bake 35 to 40 minutes or until golden and firm to the touch. Cool completely before removing side of pan. Store in tightly covered container.   *Makes 12 slices*

sugar plum cookie tree

Making these colorful edible trees will add to your holiday fun!

Colorful Sugar Cutouts (page 18)
Decorator's Icing (recipe follows)
Several drops green food coloring
"M&M's"® Semi-Sweet Chocolate Mini Baking Bits
Powdered sugar

To prepare cookies make recipe for **Colorful Sugar Cutouts** as directed. Using star-shaped cookie cutters in 5 graduated sizes, cut 3 cookies from each of the four largest stars and 4 cookies from the smallest star, making a total of 16 star-shaped cookies. Bake and cool as directed.

To decorate cookies: Using **Decorator's Icing** ice both sides of one of the smallest stars; set aside to dry. To remaining icing, add green food coloring until mixture is of desired color. Ice one side of remaining 15 star-shaped cookies; let dry.

To assemble tree: Place one of the largest stars on serving platter. Begin stacking remaining stars from largest to smallest, using small dab of icing to secure in place; alternate position of points of each star as stacking continues to create tree. Top tree with solid white star. Decorate tree by placing "M&M's"® Semi-Sweet Chocolate Mini Baking Bits on all tree branches to create lights; secure with additional dabs of icing. Dust tree lightly with powdered sugar to create "snow."

Makes one 9-inch cookie tree

DECORATOR'S ICING: In mixing bowl with electric beaters beat 3 egg whites and ¼ teaspoon cream of tartar until foamy. Gradually add 1 pound (about 4 cups) powdered sugar, continuing to beat mixture at high speed 4 to 7 minutes or until of spreading consistency. (Note—if mixture is too thick, add water, 1 tablespoon at a time, until mixture is of desired consistency.) Keep bowl covered with damp cloth as icing will dry quickly.

sugar plum cookie tree

jeweled brownie cheesecake

"M&M's"® Chocolate Mini Baking Bits, fudgy brownies and creamy cheesecake are all in this one great dessert!

¾ cup (1½ sticks) butter or margarine
4 squares (1 ounce each) unsweetened baking chocolate
1½ cups granulated sugar
4 large eggs, divided
1 cup all-purpose flour
1¾ cups "M&M's"® Chocolate Mini Baking Bits, divided
½ cup chopped walnuts, optional
1 8-ounce package cream cheese, softened
1 teaspoon vanilla extract

Preheat oven to 350°F. Lightly grease 9-inch springform pan; set aside. Place butter and chocolate in large microwave-safe bowl. Microwave on HIGH 1 minute; stir. Microwave on HIGH an additional 30 seconds; stir until chocolate is completely melted. Add sugar and *3 eggs,* one at a time, beating well after each addition; blend in flour. Stir in *1¼ cups "M&M's"® Chocolate Mini Baking Bits* and nuts, if using; set aside. In large bowl beat cream cheese, remaining *1 egg* and vanilla. Spread half of the chocolate mixture into prepared pan. Carefully spread cream cheese mixture evenly over chocolate mixture, leaving 1-inch border. Spread remaining chocolate mixture evenly over top, all the way to the edges. Sprinkle with remaining *½ cup "M&M's"® Chocolate Mini Baking Bits.* Bake 40 to 45 minutes or until firm to the touch. Cool completely. Store in refrigerator in tightly covered container. *Makes 12 slices*

jeweled brownie cheesecake

chocolate iced shortbread

Two tastes of chocolate make these colorful treats great for any occasion!

1 cup (2 sticks) butter or margarine, softened
½ cup granulated sugar
1 teaspoon vanilla extract
2 cups all-purpose flour
1¾ cups "M&M's"® Semi-Sweet Chocolate Mini Baking Bits, divided
1 cup prepared chocolate frosting

Preheat oven to 350°F. Lightly grease 13×9×2-inch baking pan. In large bowl cream butter, sugar and vanilla until light and fluffy. Add flour; mix to form stiff dough. Stir in *1 cup "M&M's"® Semi-Sweet Chocolate Mini Baking Bits.* Press dough into prepared pan. Bake 18 to 20 minutes or until firm. Cool completely. Spread with chocolate frosting; sprinkle with remaining ¾ *cup "M&M's"® Semi-Sweet Chocolate Mini Baking Bits.* Cut into bars. Store in tightly covered container. *Makes 32 bars*

chocolate iced shortbread

bird's nest cookies

These little nests filled with colorful chocolate "eggs" are perfect for spring baking treats.

1⅓ cups (3½ ounces) flaked coconut
1 cup (2 sticks) butter or margarine, softened
½ cup granulated sugar
1 large egg
½ teaspoon vanilla extract
2 cups all-purpose flour
¾ teaspoon salt
1¾ cups "M&M's"® Semi-Sweet Chocolate Mini Baking Bits, divided

Preheat oven to 300°F. Spread coconut on ungreased cookie sheet. Toast in oven, stirring occasionally, until coconut just begins to turn light golden, about 25 minutes. Remove coconut from cookie sheet; set aside. *Increase oven temperature to 350°F.* In large bowl cream butter and sugar until light and fluffy; beat in egg and vanilla. In medium bowl combine flour and salt; blend into creamed mixture. Stir in *1 cup "M&M's"® Semi-Sweet Chocolate Mini Baking Bits.* Form dough into 1¼-inch balls. Roll heavily in toasted coconut. Place 2 inches apart on lightly greased cookie sheets. Make indentation in center of each cookie with thumb. Bake 12 to 14 minutes or until coconut is golden brown. Remove cookies to wire racks; immediately fill indentations with remaining *"M&M's"® Semi-Sweet Chocolate Mini Baking Bits,* using scant teaspoonful for each cookie. Cool completely.

Makes about 3 dozen cookies

bird's nest cookies

kids' favorites

brownie turtle cookies

These chewy little turtles are as fun to eat as they are to make!

  2 squares (1 ounce each) unsweetened baking chocolate
 ⅓ cup solid vegetable shortening
  1 cup granulated sugar
 ½ teaspoon vanilla extract
  2 large eggs
1¼ cups all-purpose flour
 ½ teaspoon baking powder
 ½ teaspoon salt
  1 cup "M&M's"® Milk Chocolate Mini Baking Bits, divided
  1 cup pecan halves
 ⅓ cup caramel ice cream topping
 ⅓ cup shredded coconut
 ⅓ cup finely chopped pecans

Preheat oven to 350°F. Lightly grease cookie sheets; set aside. Heat chocolate and shortening in 2-quart saucepan over low heat, stirring constantly until melted; remove from heat. Mix in sugar, vanilla and eggs. Blend in flour, baking powder and salt. Stir in *⅔ cup "M&M's"® Milk Chocolate Mini Baking Bits.* For each cookie, arrange 3 pecan halves, with ends almost touching at center, on prepared cookie sheets. Drop dough by rounded teaspoonfuls onto center of each group of pecans; mound the dough slightly. Bake 8 to 10 minutes just until set. *Do not overbake.* Cool completely on wire racks. In small bowl combine ice cream topping, coconut and nuts; top each cookie with about 1½ teaspoons mixture. Press remaining *⅓ cup "M&M's"® Milk Chocolate Mini Baking Bits* into topping on each cookie.

Makes about 2½ dozen cookies

brownie turtle cookies

pb & j cookie sandwiches

Imagine having all your favorite tastes—milk chocolate, peanut butter and jelly—rolled into one great snack!

½ **cup butter or margarine, softened**
½ **cup creamy peanut butter**
¼ **cup solid vegetable shortening**
1 **cup firmly packed light brown sugar**
1 **large egg**
1 **teaspoon vanilla extract**
1⅔ **cups all-purpose flour**
1 **teaspoon baking soda**
½ **teaspoon baking powder**
1 **cup "M&M's"® Milk Chocolate Mini Baking Bits**
½ **cup finely chopped peanuts**
½ **cup grape or strawberry jam**

Preheat oven to 350°F. In large bowl cream butter, peanut butter, shortening and sugar until light and fluffy; beat in egg and vanilla. In medium bowl combine flour, baking soda and baking powder; blend into creamed mixture. Stir in "M&M's"® Milk Chocolate Mini Baking Bits and nuts. Drop by rounded teaspoonfuls onto ungreased cookie sheets. Bake 8 to 10 minutes or until light golden. Let cool 2 minutes on cookie sheets; remove to wire racks to cool completely. Just before serving, spread ½ teaspoon jam on bottom of one cookie; top with second cookie. Store in tightly covered container.   *Makes about 2 dozen sandwich cookies*

pb & j cookie sandwiches

ultimate rocky road cups

Everyone will love the colorful twist "M&M's"® Chocolate Mini Baking Bits add to this favorite taste in brownies!

¾ cup (1½ sticks) butter or margarine
4 squares (1 ounce each) unsweetened baking chocolate
1½ cups granulated sugar
3 large eggs
1 cup all-purpose flour
1¾ cups "M&M's"® Chocolate Mini Baking Bits
¾ cup coarsely chopped peanuts
1 cup mini marshmallows

Preheat oven to 350°F. Generously grease 24 (2½-inch) muffin cups or line with foil liners. Place butter and chocolate in large microwave-safe bowl. Microwave on HIGH 1 minute; stir. Microwave on HIGH an additional 30 seconds; stir until chocolate is completely melted. Add sugar and eggs, one at a time, beating well after each addition; blend in flour. In separate bowl combine "M&M's"® Chocolate Mini Baking Bits and nuts; stir 1 cup baking bits mixture into brownie batter. Divide batter evenly among prepared muffin cups. Bake 20 minutes. Combine remaining baking bits mixture with marshmallows; divide evenly among muffin cups, topping hot brownies. Return to oven; bake 5 minutes longer. Cool completely before removing from muffin cups. Store in tightly covered container. *Makes 24 cups*

Variations:

Mini Ultimate Rocky Road Cups: Prepare recipe as directed above, dividing batter among 60 generously greased 2-inch mini muffin cups. Bake 15 minutes. Sprinkle with topping mixture; bake 5 minutes longer. Cool completely before removing from cups. Store in tightly covered container. Makes about 60 mini cups.

Ultimate Rocky Road Squares: Prepare recipe as directed above, spreading batter into generously greased 13×9×2-inch baking pan. Bake 30 minutes. Sprinkle with topping mixture; bake 5 minutes longer. Cool completely. Cut into squares. Store in tightly covered container. Makes 24 squares.

ultimate rocky road cups

take-along snack mix

Chock-full of all good things the kids will love!

   1 tablespoon butter or margarine
   2 tablespoons honey
   1 cup toasted oat cereal, any flavor
   ½ cup coarsely broken pecans
   ½ cup thin pretzel sticks, broken in half
   ½ cup raisins
   1 cup "M&M's"® Chocolate Mini Baking Bits

In large heavy skillet over low heat, melt butter; add honey until blended. Add cereal, nuts, pretzels and raisins, stirring until all pieces are evenly coated. Continue cooking over low heat about 10 minutes, stirring frequently. Remove from heat; immediately spread on waxed paper until cool. Add "M&M's"® Chocolate Mini Baking Bits. Store in tightly covered container.

Makes about 3½ cups

peanut butter crispy treats

Colorful chocolate baking bits add a delightful crunch and milk chocolate flavor to these no-bake treats.

   4 cups toasted rice cereal
   1¾ cups "M&M's"® Milk Chocolate Mini Baking Bits
   4 cups mini marshmallows
   ½ cup creamy peanut butter
   ¼ cup butter or margarine
   ⅛ teaspoon salt

Combine cereal and "M&M's"® Milk Chocolate Mini Baking Bits in lightly greased baking pan; set aside. Melt marshmallows, peanut butter, butter and salt in heavy saucepan over low heat, stirring occasionally until mixture is smooth. Pour melted mixture over cereal mixture, tossing lightly until thoroughly coated. Gently shape into 1½-inch balls with buttered fingers. Place on waxed paper; cool at room temperature until set. Store in tightly covered container. *Makes about 3 dozen*

Variation: *After cereal mixture is thoroughly coated, press lightly into greased 13×9×2-inch pan. Cool completely; cut into bars. Makes 24 bars.*

top to bottom: take-along snack mix and peanut butter crispy treats

happy cookie pops

You can't help but smile when you eat these cookie treats!

1½ cups granulated sugar
1 cup butter-flavored solid vegetable shortening
2 large eggs
1 teaspoon vanilla extract
2¾ cups all-purpose flour
1 teaspoon baking powder
½ teaspoon baking soda
1¾ cups "M&M's"® Chocolate Mini Baking Bits, divided
Additional granulated sugar
2½ dozen flat wooden ice cream sticks
Prepared frostings
Tubes of decorator's icing

In large bowl cream 1½ cups sugar and shortening until light and fluffy; beat in eggs and vanilla. In medium bowl combine flour, baking powder and baking soda; blend into creamed mixture. Stir in *1¼ cups "M&M's"® Chocolate Mini Baking Bits.* Wrap and refrigerate dough 1 hour.

Preheat oven to 375°F. Roll 1½ tablespoons dough into ball and roll in granulated sugar. Insert ice cream stick into each ball. Place about 2 inches apart onto ungreased cookie sheets; gently flatten, using bottom of small plate. On half the cookies, make a smiling face by placing some of the remaining *"M&M's"® Chocolate Mini Baking Bits* on the surface; leave other cookies for decorating after baking. Bake all cookies 10 to 12 minutes or until golden. Cool 2 minutes on cookie sheets; cool completely on wire racks. Decorate cookies as desired using frostings, decorator's icing and remaining *"M&M's"® Chocolate Mini Baking Bits.* Store in single layer in tightly covered container.   *Makes 2½ dozen cookies*

Variation: For chocolate cookies, combine ⅓ cup unsweetened cocoa powder with flour, baking powder and baking soda; continue as directed.

happy cookie pops

colorful s'mores squares

"M&M's"® Chocolate Mini Baking Bits make these squares even more fun!

½ cup (1 stick) butter or margarine, melted
1 cup granulated sugar
3 large eggs
1 teaspoon vanilla extract
2 cups graham cracker crumbs
1¾ cups "M&M's"® Chocolate Mini Baking Bits, divided
1 cup marshmallow cream

Preheat oven to 350°F. Lightly grease 13×9×2-inch pan. In large bowl cream butter and sugar until light and fluffy; beat in eggs and vanilla. Stir in graham cracker crumbs until well blended. Stir in *1 cup "M&M's"® Chocolate Mini Baking Bits.* Spread batter into prepared pan; bake 30 minutes. Dollop marshmallow cream over hot crust; spread gently and evenly over crust. Sprinkle with remaining *¾ cup "M&M's"® Chocolate Mini Baking Bits;* bake 5 minutes. Cool completely. Cut into squares.   *Makes 24 squares*

brown sugar granola cookies

These scrumptious treats combine two favorite tastes.

¾ cup (1½ sticks) butter or margarine, softened
1 cup firmly packed light brown sugar
1 large egg
1 teaspoon vanilla extract
2 cups all-purpose flour
1 teaspoon baking soda
1¾ cups "M&M's"® Chocolate Mini Baking Bits
6 KUDOS® Milk Chocolate Granola Bars Fudge, chopped

Preheat oven to 350°F. Lightly grease cookie sheets. In large bowl cream butter and sugar until light and fluffy; beat in egg and vanilla. In medium bowl combine flour and baking soda; blend into creamed mixture. Stir in "M&M's"® Chocolate Mini Baking Bits and chopped KUDOS® Milk Chocolate Granola Bars Fudge. Drop dough by tablespoonfuls onto prepared cookie sheets. Bake 11 to 13 minutes. Cool 2 to 3 minutes on cookie sheets; cool completely on wire racks.   *Makes about 3½ dozen cookies*

83

top to bottom: colorful s'mores squares and brown sugar granola cookies

quick-start treats

brownie sundae cake

*This easy and colorful ice cream cake will make
every day special.*

**1 19- to 21-ounce package fudge brownie mix, prepared
according to package directions for cake-like brownies**
1 cup "M&M's"® Semi-Sweet Chocolate Mini Baking Bits
½ cup chopped nuts, optional
1 quart vanilla ice cream, softened
¼ cup caramel or butterscotch ice cream topping

Line 2 (9-inch) round cake pans with aluminum foil, extending
slightly over edges of pans. Lightly spray bottoms with vegetable
cooking spray; set aside. Preheat oven as brownie mix package
directs. Divide brownie batter evenly between pans; sprinkle
½ cup "M&M's"® Semi-Sweet Chocolate Mini Baking Bits and ¼ cup
nuts, if using, over each pan. Bake 23 to 25 minutes or until edges
begin to pull away from sides of pan. Cool completely. Remove
layers by lifting foil from pans.

To assemble cake, place one brownie layer, topping side down in
9-inch springform pan. Carefully spread ice cream over brownie
layer; drizzle with ice cream topping. Place second brownie layer
on top of ice cream layer, topping side up; press down lightly.
Wrap in plastic wrap and freeze until firm. Remove from freezer
about 15 minutes before serving. Remove side of pan. Cut into
wedges.   *Makes 12 slices*

brownie sundae cake

orange coconut cream bars

A packaged cake mix gives these bars their quick start to a luscious treat!

1 18¼-ounce package yellow cake mix
1 cup quick-cooking or old-fashioned oats, uncooked
¾ cup chopped nuts
½ cup butter or margarine, melted
1 large egg
1 14-ounce can sweetened condensed milk
2 teaspoons grated orange zest
1 cup shredded coconut
1 cup "M&M's"® Semi-Sweet Chocolate Mini Baking Bits

Preheat oven to 375°F. Lightly grease 13×9×2-inch baking pan; set aside. In large bowl combine cake mix, oats, nuts, butter and egg until ingredients are thoroughly moistened and mixture resembles coarse crumbs. Reserve 1 cup mixture. Firmly press remaining mixture onto bottom of prepared pan; bake 10 minutes. In separate bowl combine condensed milk and orange zest; spread over baked base. Combine reserved crumb mixture, coconut and "M&M's"® Semi-Sweet Chocolate Mini Baking Bits; sprinkle evenly over condensed milk mixture and press in lightly. Continue baking 20 to 25 minutes or until golden brown. Cool completely. Cut into bars. Store in tightly covered container.   *Makes 26 bars*

orange coconut cream bars

chocolate hazelnut cookie drops

*Let your imagination run wild—use different pudding mix
flavors and nuts in these quick cookies!*

1 cup (2 sticks) butter or margarine, softened
1 cup firmly packed light brown sugar
2 large eggs
1¾ cups all-purpose flour
1 package (4-serving size) chocolate-flavor instant pudding
  mix
½ teaspoon baking soda
1¾ cups "M&M's"® Semi-Sweet Chocolate Mini Baking Bits
1 cup coarsely chopped toasted hazelnuts or filberts*

Preheat oven to 350°F. In large bowl cream butter and sugar until
light and fluffy; beat in eggs. In small bowl combine flour, pudding
mix and baking soda; blend into creamed mixture. Stir in
"M&M's"® Semi-Sweet Chocolate Mini Baking Bits and nuts. Drop
by teaspoonfuls about 2 inches apart onto ungreased cookie
sheets. Bake 8 to 10 minutes until set. *Do not overbake.* Cool
completely on wire racks. Store in tightly covered container.

Makes about 5 dozen cookies

*To toast hazelnuts, spread in single layer on baking sheet. Bake at 350°F for 7 to
10 minutes or until light golden, stirring occasionally. Remove hazelnuts from pan
and cool completely before chopping.*

polka dot macaroons

*"M&M's"® Chocolate Mini Baking Bits make
these super-easy cookies super pretty!*

1 14-ounce bag (5 cups) shredded coconut
1 14-ounce can sweetened condensed milk
½ cup all-purpose flour
1¾ cups "M&M's"® Chocolate Mini Baking Bits

Preheat oven to 350°F. Grease cookie sheets; set aside. In large
bowl combine coconut, condensed milk and flour until well
blended. Stir in "M&M's"® Chocolate Mini Baking Bits. Drop by
rounded tablespoonfuls about 2 inches apart onto prepared
cookie sheets. Bake 8 to 10 minutes or until edges are golden. Cool
completely on wire racks. Store in tightly covered container.

Makes about 5 dozen cookies

top to bottom: polka dot macaroons and chocolate hazelnut cookie drops

mini pizza cookies

A great party idea—kids will love creating and eating their very own masterpiece!

1 20-ounce tube of refrigerated sugar cookie dough
2 cups (16 ounces) prepared pink frosting
 "M&M's"® Chocolate Mini Baking Bits
 Variety of additional toppings such as shredded coconut, granola, raisins, nuts, small pretzels, snack mixes, sunflower seeds, popped corn and mini marshmallows

Preheat oven to 350°F. Lightly grease cookie sheets; set aside. Divide dough into 8 equal portions. On lightly floured surface, roll each portion of dough into ¼-inch-thick circle; place about 2 inches apart onto prepared cookie sheets. Bake 10 to 13 minutes or until golden brown on edges. Cool completely on wire racks. Spread top of each pizza with frosting; sprinkle with "M&M's"® Chocolate Mini Baking Bits and 2 or 3 suggested toppings.

Makes 8 cookies

mini pizza cookies

oatmeal brownie gems

An oatmeal crust and topping add a light crunch to these chewy brownies.

2¾ cups quick-cooking or old-fashioned oats, uncooked
1 cup all-purpose flour
1 cup firmly packed light brown sugar
1 cup coarsely chopped walnuts
1 teaspoon baking soda
1 cup butter or margarine, melted
1¾ cups "M&M's"® Semi-Sweet Chocolate Mini Baking Bits
1 19- to 21-ounce package fudge brownie mix, prepared according to package directions for fudge-like brownies

Preheat oven to 350°F. In large bowl combine oats, flour, sugar, nuts and baking soda; add butter until mixture forms coarse crumbs. Toss in "M&M's"® Semi-Sweet Chocolate Mini Baking Bits until evenly distributed. Reserve 3 cups mixture. Pat remaining mixture onto bottom of 15×10×1-inch pan to form crust. Pour prepared brownie mix over crust, carefully spreading into thin layer. Sprinkle reserved crumb mixture over top of brownie mixture; pat down lightly. Bake 25 to 30 minutes or until toothpick inserted in center comes out with moist crumbs. Cool completely. Cut into bars. Store in tightly covered container.

Makes 48 bars

Recipe for Oatmeal Brownies

From—Josephine.

Ingredients:

2 3/4 cups quick-cooking or old
    fashioned oats, uncooked
1 cup all-purpose flour
1 cup firmly packed brown sugar
1 tsp. baking soda

oatmeal brownie gems

index

index

METRIC CONVERSION CHART

VOLUME MEASUREMENTS (dry)

⅛ teaspoon = 0.5 mL

¼ teaspoon = 1 mL

½ teaspoon = 2 mL

¾ teaspoon = 4 mL

1 teaspoon = 5 mL

1 tablespoon = 15 mL

2 tablespoons = 30 mL

¼ cup = 60 mL

⅓ cup = 75 mL

½ cup = 125 mL

⅔ cup = 150 mL

¾ cup = 175 mL

1 cup = 250 mL

2 cups = 1 pint = 500 mL

3 cups = 750 mL

4 cups = 1 quart = 1 L

VOLUME MEASUREMENTS (fluid)

1 fluid ounce (2 tablespoons) = 30 mL

4 fluid ounces (½ cup) = 125 mL

8 fluid ounces (1 cup) = 250 mL

12 fluid ounces (1½ cups) = 375 mL

16 fluid ounces (2 cups) = 500 mL

WEIGHTS (mass)

½ ounce = 15 g

1 ounce = 30 g

3 ounces = 90 g

4 ounces = 120 g

8 ounces = 225 g

10 ounces = 285 g

12 ounces = 360 g

16 ounces = 1 pound = 450 g

DIMENSIONS

1/16 inch = 2 mm

⅛ inch = 3 mm

¼ inch = 6 mm

½ inch = 1.5 cm

¾ inch = 2 cm

1 inch = 2.5 cm

OVEN TEMPERATURES

250°F = 120°C

275°F = 140°C

300°F = 150°C

325°F = 160°C

350°F = 180°C

375°F = 190°C

400°F = 200°C

425°F = 220°C

450°F = 230°C

BAKING PAN SIZES

Utensil	Size in Inches/ Quarts	Metric Volume	Size in Centimeters
Baking or Cake Pan (square or rectangular)	8×8×2	2 L	20×20×5
	9×9×2	2.5 L	22×22×5
	12×8×2	3 L	30×20×5
	13×9×2	3.5 L	33×23×5
Loaf Pan	8×4×3	1.5 L	20×10×7
	9×5×3	2 L	23×13×7
Round Layer Cake Pan	8×1½	1.2 L	20×4
	9×1½	1.5 L	23×4
Pie Plate	8×1¼	750 mL	20×3
	9×1¼	1 L	23×3
Baking Dish or Casserole	1 quart	1 L	—
	1½ quart	1.5 L	—
	2 quart	2 L	—